The
UNITED
STATES
PRESIDENTS

Ronald
REAGAN

Tamara L. Britton

Big Buddy Books
An Imprint of Abdo Publishing
abdopublishing.com

abdopublishing.com

Published by Abdo Publishing, a division of ABDO, PO Box 398166, Minneapolis, Minnesota 55439. Copyright © 2017 by Abdo Consulting Group, Inc. International copyrights reserved in all countries. No part of this book may be reproduced in any form without written permission from the publisher. Big Buddy Books™ is a trademark and logo of Abdo Publishing.

Printed in the United States of America, North Mankato, Minnesota
062016
092016

 THIS BOOK CONTAINS RECYCLED MATERIALS

Design: Sarah DeYoung, Mighty Media, Inc.
Production: Mighty Media, Inc.
Editor: Paige Polinsky
Cover Photograph: Getty Images
Interior Photographs: Alamy (pp. 6, 9); AP Images (pp. 7, 17, 21, 23, 25, 27); Corbis (pp. 11, 13, 15); Getty (pp. 5, 7, 29); Public Domain (p. 19)

Cataloging-in-Publication Data

Names: Britton, Tamara L., author.
Title: Ronald Reagan / by Tamara L. Britton.
Description: Minneapolis, MN : Abdo Publishing, [2017] | Series: United States presidents | Includes bibliographical references and index.
Identifiers: LCCN 2015957557 | ISBN 9781680781144 (lib. bdg.) | ISBN 9781680775341 (ebook)
Subjects: LCSH: Reagan, Ronald, 1911-2004--Juvenile literature. | Presidents--United States--Biography--Juvenile literature. | United States--Politics and government--1981-1989--Juvenile literature.
Classification: DDC 973.927/092 [B]--dc23
LC record available at http://lccn.loc.gov/2015957557

Contents

Ronald Reagan

Ronald Reagan was the fortieth US president. Before entering **politics**, he was an actor. He made movies for Hollywood and the US military. Eventually, Reagan entered politics. He served two terms as governor of California.

Reagan was elected president in 1980. At that time, the US **economy** was very weak. But Reagan was hopeful. He wanted Americans to feel good about their country. His **slogan** was "Let's Make America Great Again!"

Timeline

1911
Ronald Wilson Reagan was born on February 6 in Tampico, Illinois.

1966
Reagan was elected governor of California.

1952
Reagan married Nancy Davis on March 4.

1981
Reagan took office as president on January 20.

1991

The **Berlin Wall** was destroyed. The **Cold War** ended.

1984

Reagan was reelected US president.

2004

Ronald Reagan died on June 5.

Illinois Boy

Ronald Wilson Reagan was born in Tampico, Illinois, on February 6, 1911. His parents were John and Nelle. In 1920, the Reagans moved to Dixon, Illinois.

Ronald played sports in school. He also acted in plays and served as class president.

★ FAST FACTS ★

Born: February 6, 1911

Wives: Jane Wyman (1917–2007), Nancy Davis (1921–2016)

Children: four

Political Party: Republican

Age at Inauguration: 69

Years Served: 1981–1989

Vice President: George H.W. Bush

Died: June 5, 2004, age 93

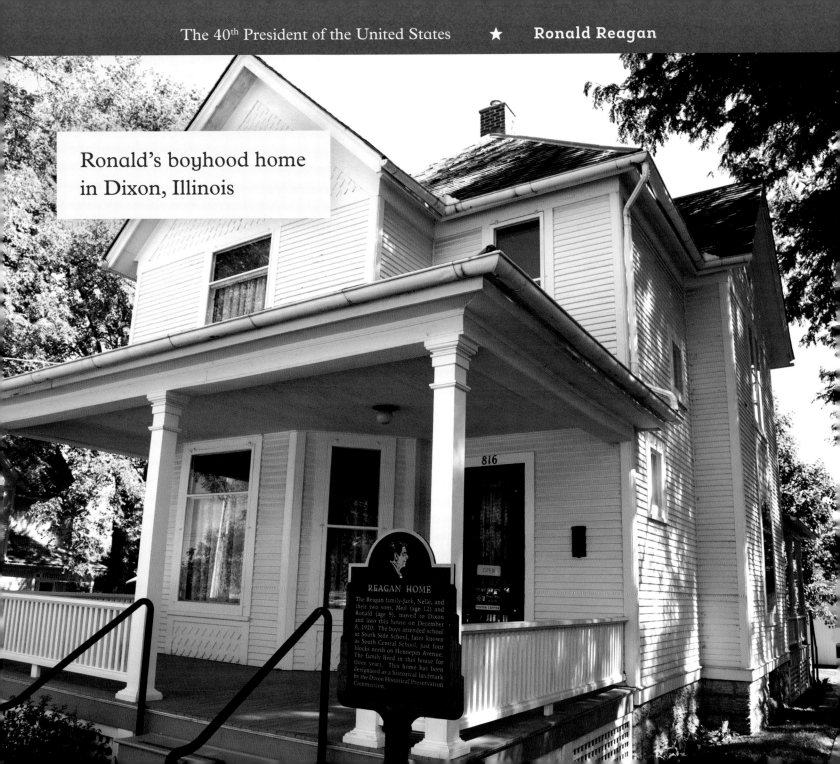

Ronald's boyhood home
in Dixon, Illinois

816

REAGAN HOME

The Reagan family—Jack, Nelle, and their two sons, Neil (age 12) and Ronald (age 9), moved to Dixon and into this house on December 6, 1920. The boys attended school at South Side School, later known as South Central School, just four blocks north on Hennepin Avenue. The family lived in this house for three years. This home has been designated as a historical landmark by the Dixon Historical Preservation Commission.

Eureka!

In 1928, Reagan began attending Eureka College in Eureka, Illinois. There, he continued to play sports and act in plays. He also helped plan a student strike. Soon after, he was elected student body president.

Reagan finished studying at Eureka in 1932. He got a job as a radio sports announcer in Iowa. But he dreamed of being an actor. In 1937, that dream came true. Warner Brothers Studios hired him as an actor!

Ronald earned ten dollars for each Iowa Hawkeye football game he announced.

Military Movies

Reagan moved to Hollywood, California. There, he met actress Jane Wyman. They married on January 26, 1940. Their daughter, Maureen, was born in 1941.

During **World War II**, Reagan joined the army. He made training movies for the Army Air Forces. Reagan's military service ended in 1945. That year, the Reagans adopted a son, Michael.

Reagan aimed to improve working conditions for actors. But, Jane was unhappy with his growing **activism**. The couple **divorced** in 1948.

Reagan and his wife Jane with their daughter, Maureen

On March 4, 1952, Reagan married actress Nancy Davis. Their daughter, Patricia, was born later that year. And in 1958, they would welcome a son, Ronald.

In 1954, Reagan began acting on a TV series for the General Electric Company (GE). Reagan spoke to GE workers across the country. From them, he learned what average Americans wanted from their government.

Reagan gave speeches about his **political** ideas. They were very popular. Reagan decided he could make a difference in politics.

(*Left to right*) Patricia, Mrs. Reagan, President Reagan, Michael, Maureen, and Ronald

Governor Reagan

After the 1940s, Reagan left the **Democratic** Party. He joined the **Republican** Party instead. Over the next 20 years, Reagan worked for several presidential campaigns.

Reagan ran for governor of California in 1966. He won by nearly 1 million votes! Governor Reagan doubled the state's education **budget**.

Reagan first ran for president in 1968. He wasn't chosen. In 1970, California reelected him as governor. Reagan ran for president again in 1976. He lost again, but his luck would change.

Reagan promised to help clean up Sacramento, California. As governor, he signed laws to improve air and water conditions.

President Reagan

In 1977, **Democrat** Jimmy Carter became president. But the country's **economy** was not doing well. Many Americans did not have jobs. In 1980, **Republicans** chose Reagan to run for president. President Carter was the Democratic choice.

Reagan asked Americans, "Are you better off than you were four years ago?" Many were not. They believed Reagan could improve the economy. On November 4, 1980, Reagan won the election.

PRESIDENT REAGAN'S CABINET

First Term
January 20, 1981–January 20, 1985

- ★ **STATE:** Alexander Haig Jr.,
  George P. Shultz (from July 16, 1982)
- ★ **TREASURY:** Donald T. Regan
- ★ **DEFENSE:** Caspar Weinberger
- ★ **ATTORNEY GENERAL:** William French Smith
- ★ **INTERIOR:** James G. Watt,
  William P. Clark (from November 21, 1983)
- ★ **AGRICULTURE:** John R. Block
- ★ **COMMERCE:** Malcolm Baldrige
- ★ **LABOR:** Raymond J. Donovan
- ★ **HEALTH AND HUMAN SERVICES:**
  Richard S. Schweiker,
  Margaret M. Heckler (from March 9, 1983)
- ★ **HOUSING AND URBAN DEVELOPMENT:**
  Samuel R. Pierce Jr.
- ★ **TRANSPORTATION:** Andrew L. Lewis Jr.,
  Elizabeth H. Dole (from February 7, 1983)
- ★ **ENERGY:** James B. Edwards,
  Donald P. Hodel (from December 8, 1982)
- ★ **EDUCATION:** Terrel H. Bell

Second Term
January 20, 1985–January 20, 1989

- ★ **STATE:** George P. Shultz
- ★ **TREASURY:** Donald T. Regan,
  James A. Baker III (from February 25, 1985),
  Nicholas F. Brady (from August 18, 1988)
- ★ **DEFENSE:** Caspar Weinberger,
  Frank Carlucci (from November 21, 1987)
- ★ **ATTORNEY GENERAL:** William French Smith,
  Edwin Meese (from February 25, 1985),
  Dick Thornburgh (from August 11, 1988)
- ★ **INTERIOR:** Donald P. Hodel
- ★ **AGRICULTURE:** John R. Block,
  Richard E. Lyng (from March 7, 1986)
- ★ **COMMERCE:** Malcolm Baldrige,
  C. William Verity (from October 19, 1987)
- ★ **LABOR:** Raymond J. Donovan,
  William E. Brock (from April 29, 1985),
  Ann McLaughlin (from December 17, 1987)
- ★ **HEALTH AND HUMAN SERVICES:**
  Margaret M. Heckler,
  Otis R. Bowen (from December 13, 1985)
- ★ **HOUSING AND URBAN DEVELOPMENT:**
  Samuel R. Pierce Jr.
- ★ **TRANSPORTATION:** Elizabeth H. Dole,
  James H. Burnley (from December 3, 1987)
- ★ **ENERGY:** John S. Herrington
- ★ **EDUCATION:** Terrel H. Bell,
  William J. Bennett (from February 7, 1985),
  Lauro F. Cavazos (from September 20, 1988)

A New Plan

Reagan became president on January 20, 1981. He cut taxes and increased military spending. This plan was called the Reagan **Revolution**. Some worried it would increase the country's **debt**. But Reagan stood by his plan.

On March 30, 1981, Reagan was attacked. John Hinckley Jr. shot him. A **bullet** struck Reagan's side.

★ SUPREME COURT ★
APPOINTMENTS

Sandra Day O'Connor: 1981

William H. Rehnquist: 1986

Antonin Scalia: 1986

Anthony M. Kennedy: 1988

Reagan was shot outside of the Washington Hill Hotel in Washington, DC. Three others were injured during the shooting.

President Reagan was rushed to a hospital. There, doctors successfully removed the **bullet**. It was only one inch (3 cm) from Reagan's heart. The country admired Reagan's bravery and spirit during his recovery.

Yet, some Americans began to doubt Reagan. The nation was in a **recession**, and some blamed the Reagan **Revolution**. Over time, the **economy** improved. The recession ended after 16 months. But the country's **debt** was growing, too.

When the president saw Mrs. Reagan at the hospital, he said, "Honey, I forgot to duck!"

Second Term

By 1984, the **economy** was strong. And on November 6 of that year, Reagan was reelected president. But in 1986, his popularity fell. Americans learned of a secret plan.

Iranian **militants** had captured Americans in Lebanon. Reagan's team wanted Iran's government to help free the Americans. So, the United States sold weapons to Iran.

In Nicaragua, **rebels** called contras were fighting their government. Reagan's team sent them money from the Iranian weapon sales.

Reagan won the election by a huge number of votes. He won every state except Minnesota.

This agreement became known as the Iran-Contra affair. Reagan said he did not know of the plan. He had not directed his team very well. For that he was sorry.

Meanwhile, the United States was involved in the **Cold War**. On June 12, 1987, Reagan gave a speech near the **Berlin Wall**. He asked Soviet Union leader Mikhail Gorbachev to tear it down.

Reagan and Gorbachev signed an agreement on December 8, 1987. It reduced the **nuclear weapons** in each country. Four years later, the Berlin Wall was destroyed. The Cold War ended. Reagan became known as the Great Communicator.

Reagan (*left*) and Gorbachev
(*right*) became good friends. On
May 2, 1992, Gorbachev visited
Reagan's California ranch.

Final Challenge

Reagan's last term ended in 1989. His family moved to California. They rode horses at their ranch. Reagan wrote books and gave speeches.

In 1994, Reagan revealed that he had **Alzheimer's disease**. He wanted to raise awareness of the condition. On June 5, 2004, Ronald Reagan died. He was 93 years old.

Ronald Reagan led the United States during a wealthy time. He worked hard to end the **Cold War**. Reagan's plans raised the country's **debt**. But his positivity brightened the world.

A military honor guard accompanied Reagan from the White House to the US Capitol before his burial.

Office of the President

Branches of Government

The US government has three branches. They are the executive, legislative, and judicial branches. Each branch has some power over the others. This is called a system of checks and balances.

★ Executive Branch

The executive branch enforces laws. It is made up of the president, the vice president, and the president's cabinet. The president represents the United States around the world. He or she also signs bills into law and leads the military.

★ Legislative Branch

The legislative branch makes laws, maintains the military, and regulates trade. It also has the power to declare war. This branch includes the Senate and the House of Representatives. Together, these two houses form Congress.

★ Judicial Branch

The judicial branch interprets laws. It is made up of district courts, courts of appeals, and the Supreme Court. District courts try cases. Sometimes people disagree with a trial's outcome. Then he or she may appeal. If a court of appeals supports the ruling, a person may appeal to the Supreme Court.

Qualifications for Office

To be president, a candidate must be at least 35 years old. The person must be a natural-born US citizen. He or she must also have lived in the United States for at least 14 years.

Electoral College

The US presidential election is an indirect election. Voters from each state choose electors. These electors represent their state in the Electoral College. Each elector has one electoral vote. Electors cast their vote for the candidate with the highest number of votes from people in their state. A candidate must receive the majority of Electoral College votes to win.

Term of Office

Each president may be elected to two four-year terms. The presidential election is held on the Tuesday after the first Monday in November. The president is sworn in on January 20 of the following year. At that time, he or she takes the oath of office. It states:

> I do solemnly swear (or affirm) that I will faithfully execute the office of President of the United States, and will to the best of my ability, preserve, protect and defend the Constitution of the United States.

Line of Succession

The Presidential Succession Act of 1947 states who becomes president if the president cannot serve. The vice president is first in the line. Next are the Speaker of the House and the President Pro Tempore of the Senate. It may happen that none of these individuals is able to serve. Then the office falls to the president's cabinet members. They would take office in the order in which each department was created:

Secretary of State

Secretary of the Treasury

Secretary of Defense

Attorney General

Secretary of the Interior

Secretary of Agriculture

Secretary of Commerce

Secretary of Labor

Secretary of Health and Human Services

Secretary of Housing and Urban Development

Secretary of Transportation

Secretary of Energy

Secretary of Education

Secretary of Veterans Affairs

Secretary of Homeland Security

Benefits

★ While in office, the president receives a salary. It is $400,000 per year. He or she lives in the White House. The president also has 24-hour Secret Service protection.

★ The president may travel on a Boeing 747 jet. This special jet is called Air Force One. It can hold 70 passengers. It has kitchens, a dining room, sleeping areas, and more. Air Force One can fly halfway around the world before needing to refuel. It can even refuel in flight!

★ When the president travels by car, he or she uses Cadillac One. It is a Cadillac Deville that has been modified. The car has heavy armor and communications systems. The president may even take Cadillac One along when visiting other countries.

★ The president also travels on a helicopter. It is called Marine One. It may also be taken along when the president visits other countries.

★ Sometimes the president needs to get away with family and friends. Camp David is the official presidential retreat. It is located in Maryland. The US Navy maintains the retreat. The US Marine Corps keeps it secure. The camp offers swimming, tennis, golf, and hiking.

★ When the president leaves office, he or she receives lifetime Secret Service protection. He or she also receives a yearly pension of $203,700. The former president also receives money for office space, supplies, and staff.

PRESIDENTS AND THEIR TERMS

PRESIDENT	PARTY	TOOK OFFICE	LEFT OFFICE	TERMS SERVED	VICE PRESIDENT
George Washington	None	April 30, 1789	March 4, 1797	Two	John Adams
John Adams	Federalist	March 4, 1797	March 4, 1801	One	Thomas Jefferson
Thomas Jefferson	Democratic-Republican	March 4, 1801	March 4, 1809	Two	Aaron Burr, George Clinton
James Madison	Democratic-Republican	March 4, 1809	March 4, 1817	Two	George Clinton, Elbridge Gerry
James Monroe	Democratic-Republican	March 4, 1817	March 4, 1825	Two	Daniel D. Tompkins
John Quincy Adams	Democratic-Republican	March 4, 1825	March 4, 1829	One	John C. Calhoun
Andrew Jackson	Democrat	March 4, 1829	March 4, 1837	Two	John C. Calhoun, Martin Van Buren
Martin Van Buren	Democrat	March 4, 1837	March 4, 1841	One	Richard M. Johnson
William H. Harrison	Whig	March 4, 1841	April 4, 1841	Died During First Term	John Tyler
John Tyler	Whig	April 6, 1841	March 4, 1845	Completed Harrison's Term	Office Vacant
James K. Polk	Democrat	March 4, 1845	March 4, 1849	One	George M. Dallas
Zachary Taylor	Whig	March 5, 1849	July 9, 1850	Died During First Term	Millard Fillmore

PRESIDENT	PARTY	TOOK OFFICE	LEFT OFFICE	TERMS SERVED	VICE PRESIDENT
Millard Fillmore	Whig	July 10, 1850	March 4, 1853	Completed Taylor's Term	Office Vacant
Franklin Pierce	Democrat	March 4, 1853	March 4, 1857	One	William R.D. King
James Buchanan	Democrat	March 4, 1857	March 4, 1861	One	John C. Breckinridge
Abraham Lincoln	Republican	March 4, 1861	April 15, 1865	Served One Term, Died During Second Term	Hannibal Hamlin, Andrew Johnson
Andrew Johnson	Democrat	April 15, 1865	March 4, 1869	Completed Lincoln's Second Term	Office Vacant
Ulysses S. Grant	Republican	March 4, 1869	March 4, 1877	Two	Schuyler Colfax, Henry Wilson
Rutherford B. Hayes	Republican	March 3, 1877	March 4, 1881	One	William A. Wheeler
James A. Garfield	Republican	March 4, 1881	September 19, 1881	Died During First Term	Chester Arthur
Chester Arthur	Republican	September 20, 1881	March 4, 1885	Completed Garfield's Term	Office Vacant
Grover Cleveland	Democrat	March 4, 1885	March 4, 1889	One	Thomas A. Hendricks
Benjamin Harrison	Republican	March 4, 1889	March 4, 1893	One	Levi P. Morton
Grover Cleveland	Democrat	March 4, 1893	March 4, 1897	One	Adlai E. Stevenson
William McKinley	Republican	March 4, 1897	September 14, 1901	Served One Term, Died During Second Term	Garret A. Hobart, Theodore Roosevelt

PRESIDENT	PARTY	TOOK OFFICE	LEFT OFFICE	TERMS SERVED	VICE PRESIDENT
Theodore Roosevelt	Republican	September 14, 1901	March 4, 1909	Completed McKinley's Second Term, Served One Term	Office Vacant, Charles Fairbanks
William Taft	Republican	March 4, 1909	March 4, 1913	One	James S. Sherman
Woodrow Wilson	Democrat	March 4, 1913	March 4, 1921	Two	Thomas R. Marshall
Warren G. Harding	Republican	March 4, 1921	August 2, 1923	Died During First Term	Calvin Coolidge
Calvin Coolidge	Republican	August 3, 1923	March 4, 1929	Completed Harding's Term, Served One Term	Office Vacant, Charles Dawes
Herbert Hoover	Republican	March 4, 1929	March 4, 1933	One	Charles Curtis
Franklin D. Roosevelt	Democrat	March 4, 1933	April 12, 1945	Served Three Terms, Died During Fourth Term	John Nance Garner, Henry A. Wallace, Harry S. Truman
Harry S. Truman	Democrat	April 12, 1945	January 20, 1953	Completed Roosevelt's Fourth Term, Served One Term	Office Vacant, Alben Barkley
Dwight D. Eisenhower	Republican	January 20, 1953	January 20, 1961	Two	Richard Nixon
John F. Kennedy	Democrat	January 20, 1961	November 22, 1963	Died During First Term	Lyndon B. Johnson
Lyndon B. Johnson	Democrat	November 22, 1963	January 20, 1969	Completed Kennedy's Term, Served One Term	Office Vacant, Hubert H. Humphrey
Richard Nixon	Republican	January 20, 1969	August 9, 1974	Completed First Term, Resigned During Second Term	Spiro T. Agnew, Gerald Ford

PRESIDENT	PARTY	TOOK OFFICE	LEFT OFFICE	TERMS SERVED	VICE PRESIDENT
Gerald Ford	Republican	August 9, 1974	January 20, 1977	Completed Nixon's Second Term	Nelson A. Rockefeller
Jimmy Carter	Democrat	January 20, 1977	January 20, 1981	One	Walter Mondale
Ronald Reagan	Republican	January 20, 1981	January 20, 1989	Two	George H.W. Bush
George H.W. Bush	Republican	January 20, 1989	January 20, 1993	One	Dan Quayle
Bill Clinton	Democrat	January 20, 1993	January 20, 2001	Two	Al Gore
George W. Bush	Republican	January 20, 2001	January 20, 2009	Two	Dick Cheney
Barack Obama	Democrat	January 20, 2009	January 20, 2017	Two	Joe Biden

"Life is just one grand, sweet song, so start the music." Ronald Reagan

★ WRITE TO THE PRESIDENT ★

You may write to the president at:
The White House
1600 Pennsylvania Avenue NW
Washington, DC 20500

You may e-mail the president at:
comments@whitehouse.gov

Glossary

activism—a practice that emphasizes direct action in support of or in opposition to an issue that causes disagreement.

Alzheimer's disease—an illness that causes forgetfulness, confusion, and overall mental disintegration.

Berlin Wall—a physical barrier that separated East Berlin, German Democratic Republic, from West Berlin, West Germany, from 1961 to 1989.

budget—a plan for how much money will be earned and spent during a particular period of time.

bullet—a metal object fired from a gun, usually shaped like a pointed cylinder or ball.

Cold War—a period of conflict between the United States and its allies and the Soviet Union and its allies after World War II.

debt—something owed to someone else, especially money.

Democrat—a member of the Democratic political party.

divorce—to officially end a marriage.

economy—the way that a country produces, sells, and buys goods and services.

militant—a person who is warlike or aggressively active in serving a cause.

nuclear weapon—a weapon that uses the power created by splitting atoms.

politics—the art or science of government. Something referring to politics is political. A person who is active in politics is a politician.

rebel—a person who resists authority.

recession (rih-SEH-shuhn)—a period of economic trouble. There is less buying and selling and people may be out of work.

Republican—a member of the Republican political party.

revolution—a sudden, radical, or far-reaching change in government.

slogan—a word or a phrase used to express a position, a stand, or a goal.

World War II—a war fought in Europe, Asia, and Africa from 1939 to 1945.

★ WEBSITES ★

To learn more about the US Presidents, visit **booklinks.abdopublishing.com**. These links are routinely monitored and updated to provide the most current information available.

Index